Children's Object Sermons
for the Seasons

Object Lessons Series

Bess, C. W., *Children's Object Sermons for the Seasons,* 1026-8
Bess, C. W., *Object-Centered Children's Sermons,* 0734-8
Bess, C. W., *Sparkling Object Sermons for Children,* 0824-7
Bess, C. W., & Roy DeBrand, *Bible-Centered Object Sermons for Children,* 0886-7
Biller, Tom & Martie, *Simple Object Lessons for Children,* 0793-3
Bruinsma, Sheryl, *Easy-to-Use Object Lessons,* 0832-8
Bruinsma, Sheryl, *New Object Lessons,* 0775-5
Bruinsma, Sheryl, *Object Lessons for Every Occasion,* 0994-4
Bruinsma, Sheryl, *Object Lessons for Special Days,* 0920-0
Bruinsma, Sheryl, *Object Lessons for Very Young Children,* 0956-1
Claassen, David, *Object Lessons for a Year,* 2514-1
Connelly, H. W., *47 Object Lessons for Youth Programs,* 2314-9
Coombs, Robert, *Concise Object Sermons for Children,* 2541-9
Coombs, Robert, *Enlightening Object Lessons for Children,* 2567-2
Cooper, Charlotte, *50 Object Stories for Children,* 2523-0
Cross, Luther, *Easy Object Stories,* 2502-8
Cross, Luther, *Object Lessons for Children,* 2315-7
Cross, Luther, *Story Sermons for Children,* 2328-9
De Jonge, Joanne, *More Object Lessons from Nature,* 3004-8
De Jonge, Joanne, *Object Lessons from Nature,* 2989-9
Edstrom, Lois, *Contemporary Object Lessons for Children's Church,* 3432-9
Gebhardt, Richard, & Mark Armstrong, *Object Lessons from Science Experiments,* 3811-1
Godsey, Kyle, *Object Lessons About God,* 3841-3
Hendricks, William, & Merle Den Bleyker, *Object Lessons from Sports and Games,* 4134-1
Hendricks, William, & Merle Den Bleyker, *Object Lessons That Teach Bible Truths,* 4172-4
Loeks, Mary, *Object Lessons for Children's Worship,* 5584-9
McDonald, Roderick, *Successful Object Sermons,* 6270-5
Runk, Wesley, *Object Lessons from the Bible,* 7698-6
Squyres, Greg, *Simple Object Lessons for Young Children,* 8330-3
Sullivan, Jessie, *Object Lessons and Stories for Children's Church,* 8037-1
Sullivan, Jessie, *Object Lessons with Easy-to-Find Objects,* 8190-4
Trull, Joe, *40 Object Sermons for Children,* 8831-3

Children's Object Sermons
for the Seasons

C. W. Bess

BAKER BOOK HOUSE
Grand Rapids, Michigan 49516

Published by Baker Books,
a division of Baker Book House Company
P.O. Box 6287, Grand Rapids, Michigan 49516-6287

ISBN: 0-8010-1026-8

Printed in the United States of America

Acknowledgments

Every author needs a co-worker like Shirlee (Mrs. David) Stewart. For four years she was my administrative secretary and right hand. Shirlee took the computer files of my weekly sermons for children, corrected my mistakes, organized chapters, and then loaded that final disk for the publisher. I must thank her for a splendid job.

Before the book could be published, I became missionary pastor of Immanuel Baptist Church in Wiesbaden, Germany. Thus Stephanie (Mrs. Tony) Coston joined the team and concluded the project with a final reading of the galley proofs. Her sharp eye caught many more of those elusive mistakes which so easily creep into a manuscript.

Final thanks go to the first lady in my life. My marriage mate has encouraged and challenged me in all my writings. No mistakes about Mary! She is the most loyal team member and mother of my own grown children, Craig and Kristen. I love and appreciate her more than words can express.

Contents

Part **One**
Holidays

1

Ho Hum, Nothing New

Interest Object: New calendar

Main Truth: To be happy in a new year, remember God while you are still young.

Scripture Text: What has happened before will happen again. What has been done before will be done again. There is nothing new in the whole world. . . . So remember your Creator while you are still young (Eccles. 1:9; 12:1 TEV).

Welcome to the first Sunday of a new year! This calendar reminds us of a whole new year before us. I trust that this will be a happy new year for you, but some people don't seem happy or excited at all. Indeed, they look bored. Ho hum, another year. Nothing new, nothing exciting.

Long ago a rich king grew bored with life. He had done many great things, had become famous, and was enjoying the best foods and entertainment money could buy. Still he was not happy. He studied and became known as the wisest man alive, but being smart did not help him find happiness.

This king wrote a book in the Bible known as Ecclesiastes. It is not a very happy book. The king could not find anything good to look forward to. For him life seemed to be just an endless circle of doing the same old things over and over. "There is nothing new in the whole world," he said. The sun comes up and the sun goes down. Nothing new ever happens. How depressing!

Finally, toward the end of his life, this rich old man discovered how he should have been living. He discovered God. Although God helped him to be happy late in life, the king realized how much happiness with God he had missed. He should have been enjoying all of life.

His conclusion? "So remember your Creator while you are still young." Don't wait to please God. Start early in life loving God and doing the good deeds he wants you to do.

That is a good lesson for us as we begin a new year. Remember God while you are young. Children, you can have a wonderful future with God. Don't waste your life. Begin now being happy with God.

2

A Time to Love

Interest Object: Invitation to a valentine party

Main Truth: Love is not limited to the valentine season.

Scripture Text: A new commandment I give to you, that you love one another; even as I have loved you, that you also love one another (John 13:34).

After the cold days of Christmas and before the warm days of spring, we come to a brief "in between" season which children enjoy. Adults like this special time also, even if they do not get a vacation from work. The main day of this season is February 14. The symbol is a red heart like this one. Can you tell me which holiday we mean? *(Allow responses.)*

You are correct. Everyone knows what a red heart means. A heart-shaped valentine represents love. We can send a valentine to people we love. And it is nice to receive valentines, too. So we can say that the valentine season is a good time to show our love.

This red heart is on a valentine which invites me to a Valentine's Day party. Someone loves me enough to ask me to help celebrate the day with them. What a wonderful thought.

But is this the only time of the year we can tell people we love them? On Valentine's Day we send people valentines, but do we ignore them the rest of the year and never tell them we love them? Of course not. We ought to love people all year round.

Jesus loves us very much. He taught many wonderful lessons about praying, doing good deeds, helping the poor, and loving God. But he also taught us how to love one another. Jesus often emphasized how we must love one another. And not just on special occasions or when people give us gifts.

In John 13, verse 34, Jesus tells us to love others. So his disciples would remember this lesson, Jesus called it "a new commandment." And he did not limit it to just a few special days of the year or only when we come to church. We are to love others in the same way Jesus loves us. Listen to this verse which is good for Valentine's Day and all the rest of the year.

"A new commandment I give to you, that you love one another; even as I have loved you, that you also love one another."

3

How to Love God

Interest Object: A red valentine pinned on the storyteller's lapel

Main Truth: We must love everyone.

Scripture Text: Beloved, let us love one another; for love is of God (1 John 4:7a).

 D o you see this red, heart-shaped symbol on my lapel? Everyone knows this is a valentine which represents love. Let's talk about how we love one another. The Bible says, "Beloved, let us love one another; for love is of God."

Where do we learn best how to love others? You are right. We learn to love from God. We are supposed to love one another because God loves us. But do we really have to love everyone? Yes, of course. Just because someone is different or wears different clothes is no reason for us to stop loving them. We love others no matter what they wear or how they look.

Today you notice that I am wearing a suit with this valentine pinned to my lapel. But what if this were a funny looking suit with pink and purple polka dots? That would look very strange, but you would still love me because of what I am on the inside, not how I look on the outside.

What if I were wearing a white uniform with black stripes and a number on it? Perhaps I had a ball and chain around my feet. You would recognize me as a prisoner who had been put in jail for doing wrong. Would you still love me? Yes, again you would love me.

Let me give you another example. What if my skin color were different from yours? God makes people in many different colors—red and yellow, black and white. But they are all still precious in God's sight. We still love people no matter how they look on the outside.

Let's Have a Parade!

Interest Objects: Palm branches

Main Truth: We can be happy for victories here on earth, but only in heaven will all problems and troubles be over.

Scripture Text: The next day a great crowd who had come to the feast heard that Jesus was coming to Jerusalem. So they took branches of palm trees and went out to meet him, crying, "Hosanna! Blessed is he who comes in the name of the Lord, even the King of Israel" (John 12:12–13)!

I have a great idea. Let's have a parade! When people want to celebrate something wonderful like a holiday, they plan a party complete with a parade. Crowds gather on the streets to watch the bands and guests. Perhaps the happiest parades feature soldiers returning home from battles in foreign lands. If they return as winners, we treat them as heroes.

Some parades feature the president of our country, a governor, a senator, or some other powerful leader. We honor them with a parade if they have done good things for us. Or maybe we want them to help our city, so we roll out the red carpet to welcome them.

One of the world's most famous parades took place in Jerusalem. It was not planned by the mayor or other important people; it just sort of happened. Jesus was coming to town, and the people were excited. Because he had brought a dead man named Lazarus back to life in Jericho, many people in the city were talking. They already knew Jesus could do great miracles. Wouldn't it be wonderful if Jesus would become their king?

When the people in Jerusalem saw Jesus coming in the distance, they pulled branches off the palm trees to line the roads before him. That was their way of saying, "Welcome. You are most important." Today we roll out a red carpet in a similar way.

Strange thing about that parade in Jerusalem. The friends who were so happy for Jesus shouted "Hosanna" and "We love you, Jesus" on Sunday. But soon it was all over. On Friday some of those people turned against Jesus and shouted "Crucify him!"

We call the day of that parade "Palm Sunday," and it reminds us that no party here on earth lasts forever. It's wonderful to celebrate and have fun. But we must remember that final victory will be ours only when our time in this world is over. Only in heaven will our happiness last forever.

5

From Sad to Glad

Interest Objects: A blank paper with marking pen

Main Truth: People who had been sad at the death of Jesus became glad later when they saw him alive.

Scripture Text: Then were the disciples glad, when they saw the Lord (John 20:20 KJV).

When someone we love dies, we feel very sad. On this paper I'll draw a curve which you will recognize as a sad face. We don't even need to draw eyes, a nose, or a round head. Just this one line reminds us of a sad face.

That was how the followers of Jesus felt after he died on the cross. He was dead, dead, dead. The soldiers had done their job well. Everyone agreed that Jesus had died. So they buried his body in a sealed tomb.

It was the end. Everyone who loved Jesus was so sad. *Jesus will never be alive again,* they thought.

But wait. Did Jesus stay dead? No! He came alive! Jesus was greater than death. When his disciples saw him alive, their hearts became happy again. The Bible tells us, "Then were the disciples glad, when they saw the Lord."

Let's turn this sad face line upside down. Now look! The sad face is glad. And it all changed when the disciples saw Jesus. Jesus has the power to make us happy.

Looking to Jesus

Interest Object: A compass

Main Truth: Just as a compass always points north, so we always look to Jesus.

Scripture Text: Let us keep our eyes fixed on Jesus, on whom our faith depends from beginning to end. He did not give up because of the cross (Heb. 12:2 TEV).

Have you ever been lost in the middle of a dark woods? Or have your parents ever gotten lost while driving in a strange city? What a lonely feeling it is when you are trying to find your way in an unfamiliar place. We need help with directions, and this compass can help us because it always points north.

Notice that a colorful needle sort of floats inside this circle as a pointer. No matter how we turn it, the compass always points north. So we turn it around until the pointer is on the "N" which stands for north. When you know one direction like north, you can be sure that south is the opposite way. Hikers out in the woods can always keep headed in a straight line instead of walking around in circles.

The compass never tricks us. It always points north. In the same way, we must always look to Jesus who is our hope and direction in this world. The Bible says we should fix our eyes on him. We should keep looking at the one who loved us enough to die on the cross for us.

Easter is the season when we think about the cross where Jesus died for us. The cross helps point us toward God. God loves us so much that he died on the cross to pay for all our wrongs. But that's not all. He came alive so that we could also come alive after death. "Let us keep our eyes fixed on Jesus."

Jesus is our hope for life. Just as the compass gives directions to those who are wandering in this world, so Jesus on the cross provides direction to heaven. The cross is a compass for us during this Easter season.

7

Thank You, Mother!

Interest Object: A Mother's Day card

Main Truth: Mother deserves thanks for
   teaching us about God.

Scripture Text: I am reminded of your sincere
   ˙ faith, a faith that dwelt first in your grandmother Lois and your mother Eunice and
   now, I am sure, dwells in you (2 Tim. 1:5).

On Mother's Day we like to do something
extra for that special lady in our lives. Perhaps some
of you gave your mom a Mother's Day card like this
one. Or maybe you fixed breakfast for her and served
it to her in bed. Perhaps some of you drew a picture
and colored it very carefully and gave it to your
mom. Others of you may have bought something
from the store.

All of these are good ways to honor our mothers.
We do that because mothers give us love, food, and
attention. The apostle Paul realized that mothers
give us something even better when they teach us
about God.

In his letter to a young preacher named Timothy, Paul remembered who first helped Timothy believe in God. It was not a priest or a neighbor. It was not a father or an uncle. For Timothy it was his mother, Eunice. And how did Eunice know about God? Timothy's mother learned about God from her mother, Lois. Lois was Timothy's grandmother.

Most of you are in church today because a parent woke you up, helped you get dressed, and then brought you safely here. Most often that parent is a mother. So we give her a gift. But first we should say those simple words, "Thank you, Mother!"

A word of thanks is the first good gift you can give your mother. She appreciates your thinking of her. A gift would be nice, too. But the magic words "Thank you, Mother" should be the first gift you give. No expensive gift can replace those words.

Beginnings

Interest Object: Graduate in cap and gown

Main Truth: Graduation is not the end but the beginning of something new and better.

Scripture Text: In the beginning God created the heavens and the earth (Gen. 1:1).

Every year around this time young people get excited about the end of school. Seniors look forward to a big event called "graduation." This new graduate wearing a funny cap and long gown is ready for the graduation service. After years of hard work and study, (he/she) is ready to finish.

Graduation! What a wonderful thought. Graduation means the end of long years in study. No more bus stops or car pools to school. No more lessons. No more homework. No more tests. No more teachers. No more school cafeteria. Graduation is "The End."

But is it really the end? After we finish high school, we might go to college, or join the army, or begin working. Whatever comes next, it will be something different from high school.

So graduation is not the end but the beginning of something. That is why many schools describe the graduation service as commencement. The word means beginning. But how can we make this beginning something wonderful in our lives?

The Bible is our book of beginnings. It describes many different types of beginnings like the beginning of the world, the first people God created, the first garden, and even the first time Adam and Eve disobeyed God. The book of beginnings begins with the words "In the beginning." So we know God is very interested in beginnings. He is also concerned with helping us have a wonderful life here on earth.

Let's think of graduation or the end of school as a beginning. Whenever we start something new, it starts best with God. If we leave God out, then something is wrong. God is the God of beginnings.

Partners Together

> **Interest Object:** Pencil
>
> **Main Truth:** Many people are needed to work together as partners in God's business.
>
> **Scripture Text:** I thank my God in all my remembrance of you . . . thankful for your partnership in the gospel (Phil. 1:3–5).

On this Labor Day weekend, let's talk about working or laboring together as partners. Here is a pencil. Millions of pencils are made and sold every year. We use them at school, at home, in church, and just about everywhere. A pencil does not look very complicated. We need no instructions on how to use one. It is a very simple product to use and enjoy.

But a pencil is not a simple product for any one person working alone to make. This little product requires thousands of different people all over the world working together as pencil-making partners. Let me explain.

To make pencils we first need wood, so lumber-jacks cut trees in the state of Washington. We're glad those good laborers worked together to provide the wood. But they were not the only partners in this process.

The lead inside a pencil is called graphite, and much of our graphite comes from South America. Thousands of miners work hard to provide the stuff inside this stick.

Every pencil needs an eraser, so workmen on a rubber plantation in Malaysia do their part. Because they cooperated together, we can rub out our mistakes.

A pencil needs to be painted a pretty color, so people in Texas drill for oil. Then someone else in a refinery makes paint from the oil.

So you see, it takes thousands of people all over the world cooperating to make millions of pencils. They are partners in the process. No one person does it all. It is a job too big for even a few people.

The apostle Paul wrote a letter to church members in Philippi. He began by thanking God for them. He was especially glad for their partnership with him in the gospel. No one alone can do all of God's work.

God still wants us to be partners with him in the greatest work of all. When we become part of God's church, we are joined in the wonderful work of making disciples. That is God's plan, and he shares the joy of that job with us! What a happy thought for Labor Day.

10

The Same Old Book

Interest Objects: The same book in two different printings or editions

Main Truth: Don't be fooled by outside appearance.

Scripture Text: A new heart I will give you, and a new spirit I will put within you (Ezek. 36:26).

(Note: For this lesson you will need the same book in two different printings or editions. You might choose an old classic like *Pilgrim's Progress* or *In His Steps* from your own bookshelf. These popular works are reissued nearly every year in different sizes and a variety of covers. Begin by holding the two books together with the newer edition on top.)

A return to school each fall means we get back to the books. Here's a brand new book I just bought. The title is _____. Everyone agrees that it is a wonderful book to read and study. But something seemed vaguely familiar about this book. I didn't recognize the outside cover but the inside contents really rang a bell. I was absolutely certain I had read this book before.

Sure enough. I looked on my library shelf, and there it was. The same title, the same author, same book. But they look so different. I was fooled by outside appearance. I thought this was something new, but it was the same old book just dressed up in a new cover.

Some people say you can't tell a book by its cover. How true. The cover of a book is like a dress or a suit of clothes. Every so often the people who publish these books like to change the looks of a good selling book. What may have been a popular color or design years ago now looks old-fashioned. So they dress up the outside with brighter colors and a new picture. The book then looks very different from this old book. Yet the only thing changed was the outside cover.

We should not be fooled by outside appearance. Publishers can put a new cover on an old book, but the inside remains old. It is no better because nothing inside changed.

People are like books. The outside is not as important as the inside. We can dress in nice clothes but still be mean and rotten inside. A new dress or haircut might make us look better to other people, but God knows that nothing has changed until we change inside. God is willing to help us change for the better by giving us a new heart. An Old Testament prophet named Ezekiel understood this truth long ago when God gave him this message—"A new heart I will give you, and a new spirit I will put within you."

That is what we need to be: new on the inside—a new heart and a new spirit.

Tiger by the Tail

Interest Object: A tiger tail or colorful rope

Main Truth: It is easier to grab trouble than to let go.

Scripture Text: And lead us not into temptation, but deliver us from evil (Matt. 6:13).

Halloween is the time of year when we disguise ourselves with a mask or costume to go out at night. Maybe we dress like a tiger. We ring a doorbell and shout "Trick or treat!" That means, "Give me a treat like candy or I'll play a trick on you." Some children even do bad things that night. After all, no one can recognize them. So Halloween becomes the occasion for doing bad.

Today let's talk about a boy who was tempted to do something bad. He was walking along in the forest one day and saw a tiger asleep under a tree, a big beautiful animal all stretched out for a quiet snooze. Every once in a while the tiger's tail would twitch. That fascinated the boy.

I wonder what would happen if I grabbed that tail and gave the tiger a good tug? the boy thought. Is it right to pull a tiger by the tail? Do we really want to bother a sleeping tiger? That doesn't sound like a very good idea to me. Something bad could happen.

But the boy didn't think much about the danger. To him it was just a temptation to do something funny. So he grabbed the tiger by its tail and pulled real hard. Perhaps you can guess what happened next. The tiger tried to turn around with the boy holding on to his tail. Around and around they both went.

At first the boy thought it was very funny. The tiger was chasing him in a circle and could not catch him. But as the boy began to get tired, a terrible thought occurred to him. How would he let go of the tiger? And what would happen to the boy when the tiger was loose?

You and I don't often see tigers sleeping along the trail. But many times each day we are faced with temptations to do something wrong. Then we find it hard to get away from our bad deed. We can't easily let go because the bad deed then seems to follow us!

Jesus taught us to pray that God would lead us not into temptation but into good paths. That is good advice from a good teacher. The next time you are tempted to do something bad, remember this prayer Jesus gave us: "And lead us not into temptation, but deliver us from evil."

12

Give Thanks

Interest Object: A model airplane

Main Truth: We need not wait until Thanksgiving Day to give thanks to God because anytime is a good time to give thanks to him.

Scripture Text: It is good to give thanks to the LORD (Ps. 92:1).

This model airplane reminds us that people want to be home for holidays like Thanksgiving. The airports are filled with crowds of travelers the day before the celebration. People eagerly pack those airplanes and can't wait to arrive home. *It will be so wonderful to observe Thanksgiving Day with family,* they think.

But what if something happens while the pilot is flying the airplane? Perhaps there is a bad storm. Everyone gets scared that the airplane will crash. The pilot fights desperately to glide the airplane down to the ground. He hopes to find a flat space without trees. Maybe he can make it to an airport where fire trucks and ambulances wait for the crippled craft.

Let's pretend that the pilot is able to land in a pasture. The plane hits hard and finally bounces to a stop. Everyone tries to leave at once. Flight attendants help passengers climb out the windows and down the sliding board to safety. Finally everyone is off the plane and safe.

Now here is the question. What is the first thing those people ought to do? Of course, you know the answer in this season of thanksgiving. Psalm 92:1 says, "It is good to give thanks to the LORD." We need not wait until Thanksgiving Day. Whenever we are thankful, we should stop right then and give thanks. We can be on an airplane, at home, up in a tree, in a hospital bed, or in church.

Thanking God is a good way to worship him. Not just on Sunday but every day we can stop to thank God in prayer.

13

The Gift I Deserve?

Interest Object: Christmas gift for pastor

Main Truth: As wrongdoers we deserve death, but God gives us life.

Scripture Texts: All have sinned and fall short of the glory of God (Rom. 3:23 KJV). For the wages of sin is death, but the free gift of God is eternal life in Christ Jesus our Lord (Rom. 6:23 KJV).

With Christmas coming closer, I wonder just how many of you children are being good. I certainly am staying on my best behavior so I can get lots of good gifts. I won't do anything bad. For being so good, I deserve the best gifts. So I want what I deserve.

Ah, here comes someone carrying a beautiful Christmas package. Could this be for me? Wonderful! Isn't this timely? Just as we are thinking about what I deserve, here it comes to me. Strange. The box is not very heavy. Listen as I shake it. Well, that's unusual. We can't hear anything moving around inside. Shall I open it now? (With the enthusiastic consent of all

34

children, the pastor opens the package. A look of bewildered confusion appears on his face.)

How strange. It's empty except for this piece of paper with two Bible references on it. Let's look up Romans 3:23 and Romans 6:23. Maybe this is a clue to what I deserve for Christmas. Oops! This verse says that all of us do wrong things, and this one says we deserve to die. Instead of being basically kind and loving, we are just the opposite. Unlike God, who is good, we do bad things and deserve punishment. If we received what we deserve, then it would be death. But God loves us very much. He offers us the gift of eternal life through Christ Jesus.

Because Christmas is the time to give and receive gifts, it is a good occasion to think about God's greatest gift to us. Jesus is that gift. This is the season when we thank God for sending Jesus into our world. We didn't deserve to have the gift of eternal life he offers. Aren't you glad that we don't get what we deserve?

14

Gifts to Make Someone Happy

Interest Object: A wrapped package

Main Truth: Every gift can make two people happy—the giver and the receiver.

Scripture Text: There is more happiness in giving than in receiving (Acts 20:35 TEV).

Here is a package wrapped in Christmas paper. It looks like a gift for someone special. Every one of you children is probably thinking, "I wish that were a Christmas gift for me. I love receiving gifts."

Yes, indeed. If I am going to give this package to someone as a gift, it can certainly make that person very happy. Every gift has the power to bring a smile, a bit of joy to the person who receives it. We have fun just thinking about what could be inside. Then we get very excited while tearing open the gift. What a wonderful experience to receive a gift.

But did you know that this gift has the power to make someone else happy at the same time? Our Lord Jesus reminded us that there is more happiness in giving than in receiving. Let me explain.

If I want to give someone a gift, I start getting happy just thinking about it. Perhaps I make something with my own hands or go buy something special. That is fun. Then I take time to wrap the gift. That makes me happy all over again. Then comes the happiest moment when I give the gift to someone and see his or her happiness. I'm happy all over again.

So who has the most happiness from this gift? The giver! Jesus was so right. "There is more happiness in giving than in receiving."

15

The Real Light

> **Interest Object:** A Christmas star with light
>
> **Main Truth:** Jesus is the real light for all the world.
>
> **Scripture Text:** This was the real light—the light that comes into the world and shines on all mankind (John 1:9 TEV).

Christmas is a happy and bright celebration during a season of dark, cold weather. The colorful decorations with lots of bright lights help lift our spirits. Everywhere we go Christmas lights can be seen in store windows, on downtown streets, and on the lawns of our neighbors. Those are wonderful displays of light, but the most meaningful light is always reserved for the top of our Christmas tree.

When we decorate our Christmas tree at home, we often place a beautiful star on the top. Many of these stars have a light inside like this one. The light in the star reminds us of Jesus. He is the light of the world.

The Bible tells us in John's Gospel that Jesus brought light to people living in a dark world. Just before Jesus arrived, however, God sent a messenger named John the Baptist to prepare the way. He would get the attention of everyone and tell them what to expect. John told people to get ready for a visit from God. The one who was coming would be a wonderful new light from God to a dark world.

When John the Baptist began preaching about the arrival of God, some people got confused. They liked the preacher very much. They thought perhaps John was the light. After all, they could see very well that John the Baptist was a godly man on a special mission. They were so eager for a visit from God that this man looked like a god to them.

The preacher didn't want anyone to be confused. He himself was not the light that God was sending to the world. Instead, it was his job to point the way for God's light. John was just a messenger, a person like everyone else.

Perhaps you love your Sunday school teacher or your pastor. That is very good. Children deserve to have godly leaders who inspire them. But you must understand that we who teach or preach are sinners just like everyone else. Jesus is the only one who can save us or bring light to our dark world. So whenever you see the Christmas star glowing with brightness, remember that Jesus is the true light of the world.

16

Receive the Gift!

> **Interest Object:** A beautifully wrapped package
>
> **Main Truth:** A gift is free but not until we accept it.
>
> **Scripture Text:** But the free gift of God is eternal life in Christ Jesus our Lord (Rom. 6:23).

As the pastor or storyteller welcomes the children, he is interrupted by a smiling member who brings a beautiful package wrapped in Christmas paper. The donor apologizes for the interruption and asks if he or she could present the gift to a special person—the pastor! But the honoree, after first displaying happy emotions, then pauses to think. He sadly shakes his head to beg off, "No, I just don't have time now. But what do you children think? Should I take time to receive this gift?" The children are agreeable, of course. And the donor promises this presentation will take just a moment.

Then the pastor makes another excuse: "I really can't afford a nice gift today because I have no money." The donor hastily explains that a gift means something is free. All that is necessary now is for the recipient to reach out and receive. The pastor seems almost persuaded and asks the children again if this is a good idea. Naturally, they encourage him to take the gift now.

But yet another concern surfaces. Now the pastor feels that he just doesn't deserve such an honor. The generous giver tries to make the pastor understand, and by now the children are all excited for the pastor. They want him to accept the gift and open it now.

As the pastor opens his gift, he explains how the Christmas season reminds us of God's greatest gift to us—salvation through Jesus Christ. Jesus was the first Christmas present of all, and he came so we might have the free gift of eternal life. But some people delay accepting God's greatest gift of all for these same silly reasons. They are too busy or don't understand how a gift is free. God wants us to have salvation whether we deserve it or not. It's free from God. So we should receive the gift!

Christmas

Reminders of the Real Thing

Interest Object: Cookie jar filled with fake treats

Main Truth: A fake or copy can remind us of the real thing.

Scripture Text: And she gave birth to her first-born son and wrapped him in swaddling cloths, and laid him in a manger, because there was no place for them in the inn (Luke 2:7).

Look what I brought from my home. This big jar is a cookie jar. Every child loves cookies. Let's look inside to see if there is anything for us.

Yes, look what we have here. A whole handful of cookies. Does anyone want a treat? (Pastor or teacher allows the first volunteer to take a cookie which proves to be fake.)

You had your hopes raised, didn't you? But I should know better than to try to fool a child with a fake cookie. You can tell by looking at these cookies that they are not real. They are only copies or reminders of the real thing. They are not good to eat.

42

During this Christmas season we often see something else which is not real. We may see a manger scene with baby Jesus in it. But when we get up close, we realize that the baby Jesus is simply a doll. This is not a real manger scene. Yet that does not discourage us because we know that there once was a real manger scene with a real baby Jesus. The fake manger scene reminds us of the real one. If there had not been a real baby Jesus, then we would not have an artificial manger scene.

We have many wonderful fairy tales and stories about Christmas that are not true. But we know Jesus is real! He was born in a crowded world with no place to lay his head except in a crib or manger filled with hay. Hay is what the animals eat for food, but on that night long ago the hay became a bed for Jesus. The new parents wrapped their baby in cloth rags so he would be warm. Then they laid him in the hay to sleep.

The next time you see a manger scene, remember this verse about the night Jesus was born: "And she gave birth to her first-born son and wrapped him in swaddling cloths, and laid him in a manger, because there was no place for them in the inn."

18

The Reason for the Season

Interest Objects: A clock, a calendar, a few Christmas decorations, Christmas lights, holly, and small gifts

Main Truth: Let us remember that Jesus is the reason we celebrate Christmas.

Scripture Text: No one can deny how great is the secret of our religion: He appeared in human form (1 Tim. 3:16 TEV).

I s it about time for Christmas? Let's look inside my sermon sack for some objects which can help us tell time and understand the proper seasons. Here is a clock. This measures time by hours, minutes, and even seconds.

Next we have a calendar. A calendar helps us know the day, the week, the month, and even the year. So we can understand times and seasons that way also.

But there is another way you can know the time of the year and which season we are approaching. Here are some items for a special season. You recognize these as Christmas decorations. When you start seeing these decorations in stores, then you know Christmas is coming closer.

It seems to me that each type of decoration tells a different story about Jesus. Each one can remind us not just of the season but the reason for the season. Jesus is what Christmas is all about.

Here are some Christmas lights which remind us how Jesus came to be the light of the world. At night the darkness is broken by the lights which invite us to catch the Christmas spirit.

We can place this string of lights on the Christmas tree. The tree reminds us that Jesus was crucified on a cross. A cross is made from wood such as this tree. The Bible even talks about Jesus being hung on a tree.

Here is some holly which is green all year round. It reminds us that Jesus is not dead but still alive. And here are some small gifts wrapped in colorful paper. They remind us how wise men brought gifts to the baby Jesus.

Some of us are so busy having parties and giving gifts that we forget why we celebrate Christmas. If we love Jesus, we will not forget him. Every Christmas decoration and every event in this busy time should remind us that Jesus is the reason for the season.

So there is no secret about it. Everything we see in this season has to do with Jesus and how he came to earth in the form of a baby. In 1 Timothy 3:16 we read, "No one can deny how great is the secret of our religion: He appeared in human form."

Part Two

Special Days

Promotion Day

19

Welcome to Worship!

Interest Object: A church bulletin or worship guide

Main Truth: Love is worship too.

Scripture Text: Beloved, let us love one another; for love is of God (1 John 4:7).

Welcome to worship where big people join little people, where young and old come together to worship God. Some of you may be here in church for the first time. You have been to children's worship or in nursery care before, but now you are old enough to be with the big people. Welcome to worship!

How does God want us to worship him during this church service? Let's describe some of our activities every Sunday during this hour together. Some of you can read this bulletin or worship guide which tells us what happens next. But even if you cannot read, you can still guess some of the ways we worship God.

We SING together to worship God. Nearly everyone can make a joyful noise to the Lord. It is something we can all do together. We feel better when we sing.

We PRAY together. To pray means simply talking to God. God is here, so we talk to him. We praise him in our prayers and tell him how we are feeling. We also ask his blessing.

We READ the Bible. It is the greatest book ever written and contains many truths to help us grow closer to God. The Bible has wonderful stories which encourage and inspire us. We learn how to be a friend to Jesus through the many lessons from the Bible.

We GIVE money to God. We describe our gifts as tithes and offerings. God deserves our gifts because he has been so generous in giving to us.

We LISTEN to the pastor's sermon. The sermon teaches us about God. Long before the pastor stands to preach the sermon, he has prayed and studied the Bible. His wisdom and his sermon must come from the Bible.

But there's another important thing which we do every time we gather in church. Let me give you a hint. (At this point the pastor reaches out to warmly embrace a child or two.) Can you guess what we feel with these hugs?

We LOVE. Everyone needs to be loved, and the church is the place where we can love and be loved. The Bible says in 1 John 4:7, "Beloved, let us love one another; for love is of God." Let us remember that love is a key part of our worship time together.

20

Don't Wait Too Long

> **Interest Object:** Picture or model of a Canada goose
>
> **Main Truth:** We ought to begin our preparations now for that trip to heaven before it is too late.
>
> **Scripture Text:** Behold, now is the acceptable time; behold, now is the day of salvation (2 Cor. 6:2).

Here is a lovely and graceful bird named for the country where she was hatched and calls home. She is known as the Canada goose. Can you guess where she spends her winters? No, not in Canada. During the cold winters of Canada, this beautiful bird lives in south Texas and north Mexico where the sun is warm and food is easy to find. Let's pretend we are in Texas during March or April. We see Mrs. Canada Goose gathering with all her family and friends.

"What are you doing together?" we ask. She answers: "We're leaving on a long trip. We're all flying back to our home in Canada so we can build nests and raise families."

50

"Wait a minute," we say. "Don't you know what the weather is like up there now? The weatherman on television described a big blizzard in Canada. You can't build your nest in the snow! Perhaps you ought to wait until the weather is better up there."

Mrs. Goose stares at us humans who like to put things off. "Oh, but you don't understand about our long trip up north. It may be snowing up there now. Yet, when we finally arrive in Canada, it will be spring. I have faith to believe God wants us to start now. We can't wait around."

Yes, Mrs. Goose is right. Some things won't wait. We must plan ahead. The Bible teaches us to start planning now while we are young so we can have a wonderful trip someday to our real home in heaven. If we wait until we are older before starting, it may be too late! We ought to begin now by giving ourselves to God.

Some people will admit that they want to go to heaven someday. But they just do not want to think about it now. They are too busy having fun. Or they think God will expect too much from them if they invite him into their lives. So they delay the most important decision in life. Some people like that never get around to starting their homeward journey to heaven. Then they die and miss heaven completely.

Now is the best time for us to give ourselves to Jesus. Not next year or some time way off in the future. The best time is *now*. "Behold, now is the acceptable time; behold, now is the day of salvation."

21

Until He Comes

Interest Objects: A clock and calendar

Main Truth: Rather than watch a clock or calendar while waiting for Jesus to return, we can remember him at the table of communion.

Scripture Text: For as often as you eat this bread and drink the cup, you proclaim the Lord's death until he comes (1 Cor. 11:26).

When we know someone special is coming to visit us, we get excited. Perhaps your favorite uncle is on his way to your home. You like him because he gives good hugs, tells great stories, and brings interesting gifts. Or maybe your best friend who moved away last year is coming to visit. When that friend arrives, you will go to the zoo, or go swimming, or do lots of other happy things together.

But first you must wait. And wait. And wait. It seems like forever. If you know what time your friend will arrive today, this clock can help you keep track of time. When the little hand gets to three, your parents tell you, your friend should arrive.

If the visit is more than a day off, you may need a calendar. You mark off a day every night before you go to bed. You are one day closer to that happy occasion.

The Bible tells us that the most special friend of all is Jesus. Someday he is coming back in a wonderful way. He will take us to heaven. That will be exciting. But we do not know the exact time when he will return.

How do we wait for Jesus? One good way is with the Lord's Supper at church. This special occasion is observed with a cup and bread by many churches. Sometimes it seems sad when we think how Jesus died for us. But he promised to come alive again and he did! He also promised to come back to get us and he will!

We eat this bread and drink this cup remembering how our Lord died for us. Jesus wants us to do this until he comes. By participating in this special event, we keep his memory alive. It is another way of reminding each other that Jesus loved us enough to die for us and that he is coming back again. "For as often as you eat this bread and drink the cup, you proclaim the Lord's death until he comes."

22

Don't Forget Me

Interest Object: A child's art work

Main Truth: Jesus wants us to remember him.

Scripture Text: "This is my body, which is for you. Do this in memory of me." In the same way, after the supper he took the cup and said, "This cup is God's new covenant, sealed with my blood. Whenever you drink it, do so in memory of me" (1 Cor. 11:24–25 TEV).

One bright Sunday morning, a pastor noticed one of his favorite children looking sad. Then he remembered why. This would be the last Sunday for the Smith family to be in church before they moved out of state. He would miss them—especially their four-year-old named Jay. They had enjoyed many special times together.

After worship the pastor was greeting many members and visitors at the door when he felt a little tug at his coattail. It was Jay who said, "Pastor, here is a picture for you. I colored it special with just you in mind. Keep it so you won't forget me."

54

You can be sure that pastor never forgot the child. What do you suppose he did with that gift? Perhaps he put it on his refrigerator door at home. Or maybe he framed it to hang on his office wall. Such a picture serves well as a reminder of the artist. It is a memory worth keeping.

That is what Jesus did for us on the Thursday evening before he died on the cross. His disciples were sad when he told them what would happen to him. But he left them a reminder like a picture. It was a special supper with something to eat and something to drink.

Jesus was telling them, "Let the bread help you remember how I gave my body on the cross for your sake. Let the drink remind you how I bled on the cross for you. Share this supper in memory of me. Don't forget me. As long as you eat this bread and drink this cup, you will remember me until I return."

We Christians have been sharing the supper ever since. We call it communion with Christ. The Lord's Supper reminds us to think about Jesus until he returns.

23

Tell the Good News

Interest Object: A small box of raisins

Main Truth: When we know something good, we must not remain silent, but rather tell the good news.

Scripture Text: Then they said to one another, "We are not doing right. This day is a day of good news; if we are silent and wait until the morning light, punishment will overtake us; now therefore come, let us go and tell the king's household" (2 Kings 7:9).

I hope you do not mind if I eat these delicious raisins. I was so hungry I thought I might starve. Then I found these raisins. My, they are very good!

Some of you look hungry. Let me tell you a story about some hungry beggars. Everyone in Jerusalem was starving because the enemy had surrounded the city and would let no one out. For many months God's people had been surrounded by that army. Then they ran out of food. Everyone was so hungry.

These beggars were also hungry. But because they were sick with leprosy, they were not allowed in the city where everyone huddled for safety. They figured they would die from starvation anyway, so they decided to go to the enemy camp and beg for food. They had nothing to lose. But when they arrived, all the enemy soldiers had disappeared. Sometime during the night these Syrian soldiers had heard strange sounds. God had scared them so that they left their tents and all their food behind. What a surprise for these beggars. They ate and ate until they couldn't eat anything else.

Then they started thinking about all the starving people in the city. Those people were so afraid of the Syrians that they would never come out from the safety of the walls. They would just starve to death. Shouldn't they go and tell the people that the enemy was gone and had left much food?

They realized that they were not doing the right thing by eating all the food and not telling other people about it. They must go and tell others the good news.

24

Home Missions

> **Interest Objects:** Large envelope with Bible inside
>
> **Main Truth:** God sends missionaries not just to people in faraway places but also to people here at home.
>
> **Scripture Text:** Then God said, "Mortal man, go to the people of Israel and say to them whatever I tell you to say. I am not sending you to a nation that speaks a difficult foreign language, but to the Israelites" (Ezek. 3:4–5 TEV).

Would you like to be a missionary who tells people about Jesus? This is a wonderful job (or mission) to do for Jesus. Some missionaries live in faraway lands like China or Africa. Perhaps you could name some more foreign countries where missionaries serve.

How did those missionaries know where to go? God must have led them to that foreign land to be a missionary. Let's pretend that this large envelope contains a message for us from God. On the outside of the envelope are the words "Missionary Orders

Inside." We can open this envelope to learn where God wants us to go for a special mission.

Where will God send us? We will know as soon as we open the envelope. What's this? Inside is a Bible with a ribbon marking Ezekiel 3:4 and 5. Ezekiel was a prophet or missionary for God. This must be a special clue, so let's read these verses. *(Pastor reads text.)*

Strange. I thought missionaries had to go to foreign lands where people speak different and difficult languages, but not Ezekiel. God wanted Ezekiel to be a missionary in his own country. He was a home missionary who could tell others about God in his own language.

We ought to tell our closest neighbors about God. They deserve to hear about God's love just as much as anyone else. So before we go halfway around the world to be a missionary, we should listen to God. Perhaps we need to be a missionary here at home.

25

My Card, Sir

> **Interest Object:** A small business card
>
> **Main Truth:** We should be ready and willing to help God.
>
> **Scripture Text:** Then I said, "Here am I. Send me" (Isa. 6:8).

Here is a small card like one carried by business and professional people. It usually has on it a name, an address, a telephone number, and a brief motto or promise. The motto could be, "I sell at the cheapest price," or "We fix anything we sell."

A business card helps people introduce themselves to anyone who might need their services. For example, a doctor might give you the card and say: "Here is my card. Call me at the telephone number listed on the card if you need me. I'll be happy to help you get well." So we take that card and tape it to our telephone or the refrigerator just in case we need to call that doctor.

Whenever a pastor goes to a conference or gathering of other pastors, he meets new people who might become friends. So the pastor gives the new friend a card to help that person remember the name. Almost always the pastor will then say, "Call me if I can ever help you."

That makes me wonder about these calling cards which are so helpful with names and numbers. They are meant to remind people that the name on the card is someone who is very willing to help them. But what if we meet God? What kind of calling card could we give him? It would not need our name or telephone number. God already knows us and where we live. He knows everything about us. God loved us before we were even born. Therefore, a calling card which we give to God needs something more than names or addresses. At least, we could still use the motto or promise.

What promise to God could be printed on our business card? It ought to be a promise to do whatever God wants us to do. I believe he wants to know if we belong to him. And are we willing to help God do his work in this world? Long ago God sent angels to carry messages and do some of his work. Now he uses his people instead. God is always looking for people to help others or do good deeds.

Are you willing to help God? If so, your calling card could have written on it the words of Isaiah who once met God in the temple. God wanted to know who would be willing to go and work for him. Isaiah was willing. He wanted very much to help God. If he had been carrying a calling card, it would have read, "Here am I! Send me." Those are the words he used.

Today is Missions Day. This is the occasion when we can think about doing God's work. Perhaps God wants us to become a missionary who travels to other places working for him. What a wonderful attitude of willingness. "Here am I! Send me."

26

Life-giving Blood

Interest Object: Blood drive poster
Main Truth: Blood keeps the body alive.
Scripture Text: For the life of the flesh is in the blood (Lev. 17:11).

Today at our church we are having a blood drive where medical technicians come and draw blood from volunteers. Although you children are not yet old enough to give your own blood, you are welcome to come with your parents and watch heroes giving blood so others can live.

This poster about a blood drive reminds me of a boy about your age who saw smoke coming from a house next door. He realized that his best friend might be inside, so he rushed around to his friend's window and looked in. Sure enough, his buddy was asleep, with the fire moving closer to his room. So the boy picked up a baseball bat that had been carelessly left in the yard and shattered the window glass. Then he climbed in and woke up the boy who had been stunned by smoke. Both boys just barely made it out the window when the whole room went up in flames.

The boy saved his friend's life and became a hero, but not without some blood being shed. While crawling into the house, a piece of glass had sliced into his arm. He had lost much blood by the time firemen arrived. While his friend received oxygen to clear the smoke from his lungs, the bleeding boy was given a saline solution to replace lost body fluid. But our hero needed something better. He needed blood.

The ambulance driver called ahead to the hospital, "We need lots of blood, or the patient will die." Fortunately, the hospital had blood ready in little plastic sacks. Where did it come from? From people who read a poster like this and decided to give some of their blood. So that lifesaving substance was ready at the hospital for any emergency. When the injured boy arrived, they put a needle in his arm and connected it to sacks of blood which flowed into his body. Our hero lived.

Now let's think about that. A hero gave blood to save the life of his buddy. But others gave blood so the hero could live. That means we have many heroes for this story.

Sure, it hurts a little bit for a needle to be put into your arm when you give blood. But it makes you feel so good when you know you are helping to save someone's life. The Bible explains that the "life of the [body] is in the blood."

This poster also reminds us how Jesus willingly allowed his blood to be shed on the cross that we might live forever in heaven. So don't forget that Jesus is the greatest hero of all. He gave his blood so all of us can live.

27

The Crown

Interest Object: A crown

Main Truth: Gray hair is a blessing from God, a badge of honor that deserves respect.

Scripture Text: Gray hair is a glorious crown (Prov. 16:31 TEV).

Do you like the crown I am wearing today? In ancient times a crown could be worn by only one person. If that person was a man who sat on a throne, what was he called? *(Allow responses.)* That's right—a king. A woman wearing a crown was a queen.

How do you treat someone who wears a crown? With great respect, of course. Everyone bows before the king or queen. They deserve honor and respect.

In this modern time you won't find many kings and queens living in palaces and wearing crowns. But if you look around the congregation today, many people are wearing a special crown given to them by God. You don't see one? Let me explain.

The Bible describes a special crown of glory not available to children or young people. God provides this crown only for older people. It can be worn day and night because it won't fall off the head. We could call it a crown of splendor or a glorious crown. You will understand when I read Proverbs 16:31 from a modern version: "Gray hair is a glorious crown."

What a wonderful thought. As we grow older and our hair turns gray, we need not be ashamed. Gray hair is something to be proud of, a badge of respect, a blessing from God. Today we honor all senior adults—even those with only a touch of gray hair. As the years fly by, God will continue turning their hair gray until it becomes like a glorious crown.

As you return to your seats, look for those glorious crowns. When you find one, treat it with respect. Give that person a smile and say: "You have a beautiful crown!"

28

Busy! Busy! Busy!

Interest Objects: Rocking chair and a walking cane

Main Truth: Today's senior adult is too busy for rocking chairs and walking canes.

Scripture Text: The righteous flourish like the palm tree. . . . They still bring forth fruit in old age, they are ever full of sap and green (Ps. 92:12, 14).

(Note: This message requires a few senior adult volunteers. It is easy to organize and it corrects stereotypes about later life. The humor and participation will be much appreciated.)

For this Senior Adult Day someone has left a rocking chair and a walking cane here on the platform. Is this what being a senior adult is all about? Must we use a walking cane to get to the rocking chair where we do nothing but sit and rock? Children, I see one of our senior adults walking very fast toward the microphone.

"Pastor, someone left you with the wrong props to illustrate old age. Most of us are too busy going places and doing things. In our congregation we have senior adults who love to play tennis." (With that cue a senior adult in the congregation stands to wave a tennis racquet, saying, "I still win tournaments. Anyone for tennis?") In rapid succession others stand with appropriate symbols like a golf club, a shopping bag, and a suitcase. Be sure to also include a uniformed hospital volunteer, a school crossing guard, and a hobbyist in woodworking or quilting.

"Yes, pastor, we are too busy to sit around and do nothing. It occurs to us that the people who need the rocking chairs are young mothers who rock their babies to sleep. The walking canes are good for young people who get hurt playing sports. Although we may have gray hair and a few wrinkles, we feel like trees that keep growing no matter how old they are. Pastor, do you have a Scripture passage that explains the way we feel?"

Indeed, I do. In verses twelve and fourteen of Psalm 92 is the description about how we can grow older in the Lord. The Bible teaches us that those who are righteous before God flourish like trees. "The righteous flourish like the palm tree. . . . They still bring forth fruit in old age, they are ever full of sap and green."

Part Three

Through the Year

29

Ask

Interest Object: Sack of candy

Main Truth: Don't be afraid to ask God for anything.

Scripture Text: And I tell you, Ask, and it will be given you; seek, and you will find; knock, and it will be opened to you (Luke 11:9).

(Note: As the children gather around the storyteller, they notice a cloth sack in his hands. But he makes no reference to it. Instead, he begins talking to the children about how wonderful God is. God provides for us the very best of everything. While the pastor is talking, a music minister or some other associate tiptoes through the children and whispers something in his ear. The pastor never stops with his story. He simply nods his head in silent agreement as the associate reaches into the bag. His friend retrieves a piece of candy and leaves with a look of satisfaction. As the pastor continues a second person comes from the choir or a nearby pew to repeat the process. After whispering in the pastor's ear, he or she is allowed to reach into the bag for a sweet reward. By this time the children are more than curious! A third person will likely be unnecessary because the children have figured out this sequence. The people who whisper in the pastor's ear are probably asking for candy. At this point, the pastor could make the following explanation:)

Pardon me, children, but some of you are not paying attention to the subject. But that is alright because you are very observant. You have noticed that some people have whispered into my ear. What were they asking me for? *(Allow responses.)* Correct! They wanted some candy from my sack. Did they get what they asked for? Yes, indeed! They did not pay for the candy. It was given as a gift simply because they had the faith to ask for it.

The Bible teaches us that God provides us with blessings. What if we need something? We should be willing to ask God for it. Our text says it all: "Ask, and it will be given you; seek, and you will find; knock, and it will be opened to you."

30

Up, Up, and Away

Interest Object: Picture of a hot air balloon

Main Truth: When Jesus returns to earth, we who belong to him will get a great ride up toward heaven!

Scripture Text: Then we who are alive, who are left, shall be caught up together with them in the clouds to meet the Lord in the air; and so we shall always be with the Lord (1 Thess. 4:17).

Have you ever thought about just flying away up in the clouds? Since we do not have wings, that is just a dream. But there is another way. We can ride up, up, and away in a hot air balloon. It would be fun to look down on earth while drifting across the sky amid those fluffy clouds. People who have flown in hot air balloons say the ride is so quiet and peaceful.

After Jesus came alive from the tomb and had visited his disciples, he just left them to fly toward heaven. But he did not need a balloon or airplane. Jesus just sort of floated up in the air. He promised to come back again in the same way. When he returns, we will look up into the clouds and see him coming. How exciting! But it gets better.

The people who are alive and who belong to Jesus will be caught up into the air and float toward the clouds to meet Jesus. That will be the most fun ever! We will go with Jesus to heaven, that prepared place, to be with him forever. And it all begins with that wonderful last ride as we leave this old earth. Up, up, and away!

But what happens if we die before Jesus returns? Jesus promises us that where he is, there we will be also. We won't miss that ride. In fact, Jesus will immediately take us to heaven. Then those who have already died and gone to heaven with Jesus will get to come back to meet everyone else in the air.

How do we know all this? Jesus promised to return. We can trust him. Also, Paul described some details to the Thessalonian church. We can read about it in our verse for today. "Then we who are alive, who are left, shall be caught up together with them in the clouds to meet the Lord in the air; and so we shall always be with the Lord."

31

Bloom Where You Are Planted

Interest Object: Miniature fruit from an
orange tree grown in a flower pot

Main Truth: Be happy wherever you must
live.

Scripture Text: For I have learned, in whatever state I am, to be content (Phil. 4:11).

Here are some small oranges grown on a
friend's tree. While these oranges are not large and
sweet like those growing in Florida, they are still
good to eat. Let me tell you the story about an
orange tree which never gave up.

It all began when neighbors were talking in the
front yard of my friend who at that time lived in a
northern state. They were eating some oranges.
Someone must have spit a seed into the flower bed,
because a few weeks later, a strange-looking plant
appeared. After a few months they finally recognized
it as a little orange tree. Silly thing. Everyone knows
that orange trees cannot survive cold winter weather.
That's why they must grow in warm places like
Florida or California. But the little tree seemed determined to live.

As winter approached my friend decided to dig up the little tree and replant it in a pot. That way it could be brought inside a warm house. Well, the orange tree just kept on growing until it was as big as the small pot would allow. Next year the family moved. Should they take along this determined little tree? Yes, certainly. And they were rewarded the next spring with sweet smelling blossoms which turned into small oranges.

Amazing! The little tree did not feel sorry for itself for not being born in a warm Florida field. It never complained of being confined to a flowerpot which prevented it from growing big and tall. And it surely didn't cry and scream when the family packed their possessions and moved across the country to another state. That must have been hard on the young tree to leave its familiar surroundings.

If the little tree that produced these oranges could talk, perhaps she would tell us about a favorite verse in the Bible. It was written by Paul who knew about tough times and having to move on. Paul never got angry about being poor or having to move away. Listen to his positive attitude in this wonderful verse. "Not that I complain of want; for I have learned, in whatever state I am, to be content."

The little orange tree would say "amen" to that. We must bloom where we are planted. If we trust God, we can be content wherever we live and whatever we do. Are you willing to be like Paul? If the little orange tree can be content like Paul, so can you!

32

Free Because God Pays

Interest Object: A newspaper grocery advertisement

Main Truth: All good blessings of God are free to us only because God has already paid the price.

Scripture Text: Say there! Is anyone thirsty? Come and drink—even if you have no money! Come, take your choice of wine and milk—it's all free! (Isa. 55:1 LB).

(Note: A grocery ad from a daily newspaper can be prepared by printing in large red letters FREE CANDY*. The asterisk is duplicated at the bottom of the page with the explanation "Free with $10.00 purchase." Individually wrapped candies can be given to the children as a memory maker.)

This is a newspaper advertisement with some good news about free candy at a grocery store near the church. Most people are interested in anything for free. But when it is free candy, wow! We can get very excited about this kind of offer. Let's say you hurry to the grocery store and ask for your free candy. Do you know what will happen?

The clerk will say, "But, didn't you read the fine print?" And then you look at the bottom of the page. It says that the candy is free only with a $10.00 purchase of groceries. Now you don't have any money. That means you won't get the free candy.

Let us further pretend that as you are standing there, you see a neighbor who ought to be very mad at you. Perhaps you were playing ball with some children the day before and broke his window. Most neighbors would be very angry.

But this neighbor does a wonderful thing. Instead of being angry, he calls you over and places his hand on your shoulder. He says, "I have just bought more than $10.00 worth of groceries. Because I love you, I'll ask the manager to give you the free candy which I deserve." Wouldn't that be wonderful?

Did you know that is how God deals with us? We do not deserve to have any of his free gifts, but he wants us to have the best. Therefore, he has already paid the price for us. He offers us something better than candy which will not last long. God promises to give us salvation and a home in heaven forever. All we need to do is trust him enough to invite him into our lives.

In the Old Testament a prophet named Isaiah spoke for God concerning the free gift. It's free because God has paid the price! Let's read about it in Isaiah 55:1. "Say there! Is anyone thirsty? Come and drink—even if you have no money! Come, take your choice of wine and milk—it's all free!"

33

Someone Pays

Interest Object: Coffee mug good for free coffee at participating businesses

Main Truth: Jesus is the One who paid for our gift of salvation.

Scripture Text: For the wages of sin is death, but the free gift of God is eternal life in Christ Jesus our Lord (Rom. 6:23).

Here is my favorite coffee mug. Anytime I am on the road, this special mug travels with me. You notice the emblem and colors of a famous business where you like to stop for ice cream and hamburgers. They serve good coffee. I especially enjoy their coffee because it comes free with this mug.

Everyone likes a bargain, especially something free. The coffee just tastes better to me when I don't have to pay for it.

Many different stores and gas stations have their own special mugs. If you bring these cups or mugs back to them, they refill them for a very cheap price. However, the fast food restaurant honors this mug with free coffee.

But wait a minute. The coffee I drink from this mug is not exactly free. Someone pays the people who pick the beans. Someone pays the shipper and then the processor who prepares the coffee beans. Everyone who handles the coffee beans must receive some profit so they can have money to feed their children. If I do not pay for this cup of coffee, then who does? *(Allow responses.)* You are right. The owner of the business had to buy that coffee before she could give it to me. Everything costs someone something.

The Bible explains how God offers us the free gift of salvation. He wants us to live forever. He loved us enough to die on the cross for us. That was his way of providing something for us which we could never afford or gain on our own. This is his gift to us. It is free because God has already paid the price.

34

You Are Different!

Interest Object: Cookie cutter in the form of a child

Main Truth: You're different because God made you like no one else.

Scripture Text: So God created man in his own image, in the image of God he created him; male and female he created them (Gen. 1:27).

Here is a cookie cutter which can be used to shape those delicious cookies someone bakes for you. I have traced the form on some folded paper and then cut out these paper cookies to show you how they are always identical. Ho hum, every cookie is the same. Gets boring after a while, doesn't it?

Everyone likes a little variety in life. You would not want to wear the same clothes every day, would you? That is why styles change. For variety a lady will change her hairdo and a man will buy a blue car after his red one wears out.

We can be sure that God enjoys variety in his creation. Want proof? Then look at all the different people around you. Everyone is created with different features and in different sizes and colors. God never makes two people just alike. Even identical twins born from the same parents and at the same time have differences.

The Bible describes how God created everything in the beginning. God decided to use his own image when making the first people. He made us a lot like himself. But even then, he didn't use a cookie cutter to make us exactly alike. The first two people God made were Adam and Eve. They didn't look much alike, did they?

Perhaps someone will try to make fun of you one day by saying, "You're different." The person may want you to feel weird or different in a bad sort of way. But you can remember this verse and this truth. The best way to respond is by smiling. Then you can say, "Yes, I am different. Thank you for noticing. God made me."

35

Enemies into Friends

Interest Objects: A can of grease, a can of lye, and a bar of soap

Main Truth: Enemies can become friends.

Scripture Text: But I say to you, "Love your enemies" (Matt. 5:44).

In these two cans are a couple of enemies which might be found in your home. The first fellow is Mr. Grease, who appears in a pan when we fry bacon. Mother usually pours him into a can like this where he hardens when placed in the cool refrigerator. Later she may throw him away unless he is needed to help fry eggs. The rest of the time Mr. Grease has nothing to do. Sometimes he gets into mischief if some of his drops wash off the pan and go down the drain. Mr. Grease will clog the pipes and cause the water to back up and overflow.

When that happens we call on this other fellow named Mr. Lye. He sits around with little to do just waiting until that drain gets stopped up by Mr. Grease. If we pour Mr. Lye into the drain, he will fight with Mr. Grease. They are enemies. Finally Mr. Lye wins by eating Mr. Grease. The drain is clear.

How much better if these two could be friends. Suppose we ask them what they could do together as friends instead of enemies?

Mr. Grease turns away angrily and yells: "Nothing at all!" And Mr. Lye responds, "I just don't like that fellow."

Jesus taught us that the best way to love an enemy is to love him enough so that you both become friends. And it works with these two enemies. Do you know what happens if we combine these two enemies in a proper mixture on a hot stove? We can make soap. That's like a miracle!

Look at this bar of soap. In the old days lye soap was the only thing people had for washing their hands or clothes. Some people today still think this type of old-fashioned soap is the best ever.

Isn't this an exciting thought? We put together two lazy enemies and come out with a hardworking friend like soap. Mr. Lye and Mr. Grease discover that they don't have to be enemies. They can become friends by helping each other.

Now we are ready to read the Bible for this same truth which Jesus taught us. He said, "But I say to you, 'Love your enemies.'"

36

Faithful

Interest Object: Picture of pony express rider on a horse

Main Truth: Jesus wants us to be faithful to our duties.

Scripture Text: The one thing required of such a servant is that he be faithful to his master (1 Cor. 4:2 TEV).

Make way for the mailman! Between 1860 and 1861 the most faithful mail persons were young cowboys who raced between St. Joseph, Missouri, and Sacramento, California. They never slowed down for anything. This picture shows one of those brave riders on his speedy horse. He stopped only to change ponies. If no other rider was ready after he finished his fifty-mile stretch, he kept on going without food or sleep.

Once the pony express saddlebag filled with mail left Missouri, it never stopped until the last of forty different riders had carried it for nearly 2,000 miles! The total time for that trip was only ten days.

How were they so successful? They chose the fastest ponies in the land and fed them lots of oats. Horses which ate a good breakfast could easily outrun the Indian ponies which only ate grass. (Children need good food to do their best, also!)

Small young men were chosen as riders so the horse would not be slowed by a heavy load. The saddle was very small and thin. To save even more weight, the cowboy carried no weapons. When chased he had to outrun his enemies instead of stopping to fight. The pony express rider promised to keep going without stopping.

Yes, the pony express rider was always faithful. He remembered the people who wrote those letters. He remembered those who wanted to receive those letters. And he was also faithful to his company which promised to get those letters delivered. He was the best kind of servant possible.

The Bible teaches us to be good servants for Jesus. He is our master or boss. We must promise to follow him if we want to be his servants. So the most important thing we can do for Jesus is to be like the pony express riders who were always faithful.

They remind us of the truth found in 1 Corinthians: "The one thing required of such a servant is that he be faithful to his master."

37

The Perfect Giver

Interest Object: Birdseed

Main Truth: God is the perfect giver of all gifts because he never changes his mind about being so generous.

Scripture Text: Every good gift and every perfect present comes from heaven; it comes down from God, the Creator of the heavenly lights, who does not change (James 1:17 TEV).

In our sermon sack today is some food for a big crowd of guests at my house. It seems that we are always having company. They fly in from all over the country and enjoy the food which we provide them. I believe they could eat us out of house and home—except we don't let them in our house. We feed them in the backyard!

You wonder what kind of company I feed in the backyard? Let's look in the sack to find out. Who would eat these seeds? *(Allow responses.)* You're right. This is birdseed.

You should see the beautiful birds coming to my backyard. We enjoy watching them even if they never express appreciation for the handout. Sometimes I wonder if they realize that I'm the one who gives them such good food. They never thank me.

Of course, sometimes we get busy and forget to fill their bird feeder. Other times we may go out of town and they go hungry again. Then in the autumn season when lots of berries and other seeds are abundant in the woods, the birds aren't as interested in my food. That sort of disappoints me. One October I stopped filling their feeder for a whole week. *That will teach them,* I thought!

That doesn't make me sound loving or gracious, does it? I am not a perfect provider. Sometimes I forget and other times I get angry. I'm glad God does not act like that. The Bible teaches us that every good gift and every perfect present on earth comes down out of heaven from God. He gives and gives and gives. He never changes his mind or his attitude about loving us and providing for us. The perfect giver does not change!

James described God in his giving ways: "Every good gift and every perfect present comes from heaven; it comes down from God, the Creator of the heavenly lights, who does not change."

Aren't you glad that God doesn't stop giving to us when we forget to thank him? He loves us always. He is the perfect giver of all gifts.

38

Broken Hearts

Interest Object: Safety helmet (hard hat)

Main Truth: Jesus heals broken hearts.

Scripture Text: He . . . sent me to heal the brokenhearted (Luke 4:18 KJV).

This is a safety helmet or a hard hat. It is similar to those worn by football players or motorcyclists. Construction workers who build new highways or buildings wear these hard hats. Why? They don't want to be hurt when objects fall on top of them from high above the project.

Let me show you how this hard hat protects the head. We will fit it on some willing volunteer. Then we can thump the top of the hat. See! The hard hat cushions the blow and protects the head. This saves the construction worker a trip to the doctor.

But what happens when you have a broken heart? Perhaps a friend says bad things about you. Or someone you love may be very sick and even die. You have a hurt deep inside your body. A hard hat won't help when you have a broken heart.

It takes a special doctor to help us with a broken heart. The Bible tells us that Jesus came to heal those who have a hurt in the heart. That was one of the reasons Jesus came from heaven to be with us on earth.

At the beginning of his ministry, Jesus came back home to Nazareth. When the day of regular worship came, Jesus went with all the people. They asked him to read from the Bible. So he chose the Book of Isaiah.

One of the things Jesus read that day in church was this sentence. "He . . . sent me to heal the brokenhearted." That sentence describes very well what Jesus does best. When we have a hurting heart, Jesus can comfort and help us. He is the best heart doctor in the whole wide world!

39

The Mighty Mite

Interest Object: Public address microphone

Main Truth: God takes the little we give and magnifies it into a lot.

Scripture Text: Truly I say to you, this poor widow put in more than all of them (Luke 21:3).

Here is a microphone which makes my voice sound louder to those who are in the back pew. Many people call this microphone a mike. This is a wonderful invention which magnifies or amplifies sound so even the softest voice can be heard.

An older woman living in a tough neighborhood decided to buy a dog for protection. She thought that if a burglar tried to break into her house, the dog would bark and scare him off. So she bought a cute little puppy dog. Then she trained her little guard dog to bark. The only problem was that the little dog had a little bark that would never scare a mean burglar.

What could she do? She didn't want to trade her little dog for a big mean dog. Fortunately, a neighbor boy helped her solve the problem. He bought a machine with a microphone like this. Then he taught the dog to watch for a stranger. If someone knocked on her door or looked in through the window, the little dog would run to the microphone and growl. It worked well because the little growl sounded like a lion!

God can work with us in a similar way. He takes what little bit we have to offer and turns it into a lot. For example, perhaps we don't have a million dollars to place in the offering plate. But God does not need a million dollars from little people. He will take your little pennies and turn them into big blessings. God knows how to magnify our gifts.

Jesus once saw a poor old woman with only two mites. Mite sounds like mike, but in those days it was like a penny. This poor widow emptied her purse and put everything in the offering plate at church. It was only two mites, but Jesus said that was worth more than all the dollars the rich people gave.

The Fourth Little Monkey

Interest Object: Picture or model of the famous Three Little Monkeys

Main Truth: Avoiding evil does not keep us from having fun.

Scripture Text: Rejoice in the Lord always; again I will say, Rejoice (Phil. 4:4).

Do you recognize these little monkeys? The first little monkey has his hands covering his ears so he will hear no evil. The second one has covered his eyes so he will see no evil. The third little monkey uses his hands to keep his mouth closed so he will speak no evil. They look very serious and afraid. It makes us wonder if a fourth little monkey ought to join them. He would have his hands thrown up in disgust. He would be known as "Have no fun."

Is that what we learn from the Bible when we attend church? Stop doing this and don't do that. Be careful. Be serious. Does avoiding evil mean we can never have any fun?

Absolutely not! People who belong to Jesus have lots of fun. They don't have to worry about getting

94

into trouble with God. They know how much he loves us. They have fun with one another. Being a Christian means living a life filled with joy. We sing "Serve the Lord with Gladness." And we mean it because that is what the Bible teaches us.

Paul wrote to the members of the Philippian church: "Rejoice in the Lord always; again I will say, Rejoice."

Where did he learn about happiness and joy and rejoicing? He learned it from the Book of Psalms where King David declared: "Be glad in the LORD, and rejoice, O righteous, and shout for joy" (Ps. 32:11).

But the best teacher of joy was Jesus who showed us how to be happy even when people make fun of us or throw rocks our way. "Rejoice and be glad, for your reward is great in heaven, for so men persecuted the prophets who were before you" (Matt. 5:12).

The next time you see these little monkeys looking so sad, remember how much fun it is to be a follower of Jesus. When you love Jesus, you will want to avoid evil. And you will be happy about it.

41

Making Music

Interest Object: Hymnal

Main Truth: Music is God's gift to us.

Scripture Text: Sing psalms and hymns and spiritual songs with thankfulness in your hearts to God (Col. 3:16).

In church we have Bibles which contain God's Word and songbooks which contain God's music. Some little books just have the words to choruses; the bigger books are called hymnals or songbooks. Have you ever thought about how music is God's gift to us?

We make music to praise God. We take his music and give it back to him. The Bible says that we ought to "Sing psalms and hymns and spiritual songs with thankfulness in your hearts to God." There are many types of psalms and songs and music that we can make before God.

These songs or hymns sung for God have a way of lifting us up, too. We feel better when we sing. Singing is something that everyone can enjoy.

The Bible tells about using all kinds of musical instruments to praise God. These instruments can help make us feel better.

Once a king named Saul was bothered by a bad spirit which made him feel sad. So his advisors brought in a young shepherd named David who played a harp. When David ran his fingers across those harp strings, out came lovely music which helped soothe the troubled king. The sad king became glad again.

We can be grateful to God for music which is his gift to us. The next time we sing from the hymnal, you can join us. Even if you cannot read yet, just listen and enjoy the music.

42

Power

Interest Object: A large magnet

Main Truth: Just as a magnet gets its power from some electrical source, so we receive our living power from the Holy Spirit.

Scripture Text: But you shall receive power when the Holy Spirit has come upon you; and you shall be my witnesses (Acts 1:8).

I am holding one of the most fascinating toys any child can ever enjoy. This little piece of metal attracts smaller metal pieces to itself. It holds them as if they were glued or tied onto itself. This magnet is doing what magnets like to do best. Watch as these paper clips are drawn toward its invisible power. They will even jump onto the magnet. We can make a long string of metal clips because magnetic power flows from one clip to another.

Magnets are also helpful tools. They hold paper notes on a bulletin board. We use them for notes on our refrigerator doors at home. Big magnets can pick up heavy loads of metal to move them from a railroad car to a loading dock. So they are very good tools in the home or workplace.

Where does a magnet get its strange power? This metal bar was not always a powerful magnet. It received its magnetic power from an electrical source. This metal piece was magnetized in a workshop when someone connected it to an electric current. Smaller magnets can be made by striking a metal bar with another magnet or heavy metal. Sometimes buried metal is gradually magnetized by the slight electrical current found naturally in the ground.

Magnetic power is quiet, clean, and invisible. Yet we can feel the power and see its results. In the same way, God gives us a special power to be happy and to do good deeds for him. This is called Holy Spirit power. With such power we are not afraid to tell others about God. Thank God for Holy Spirit power!

We first learned about this Holy Spirit power when Jesus was leaving the disciples for his return to heaven. He promised everyone: "But you shall receive power when the Holy Spirit has come upon you; and you shall be my witnesses."

43

Prints from the Past

Interest Object: A drinking glass with greasy
fingerprints exposed by powder

Main Truth: Jesus made the most lasting
impression of all time—his nail prints!

Scripture Text: But he said unto them,
Except I see in his hands the print of the
nails, and put my finger into the print of
the nails, and thrust my hand into his side,
I will not believe (John 20:25 KJV).

Would you like to become a private
investigator or a detective? If so, then fingerprints
like those on this glass might help solve a case.

Let's pretend you are looking for someone special
who saved your life earlier in the day. That person
pushed you out of the way when a truck ran out of
control up on the sidewalk. It happened so fast that
you didn't have time to thank him properly. Now
you want to find that person and give him one million dollars as a reward, but who was he? What is
his name?

Think carefully now. Could he have left a footprint when he walked away through some mud or sand? You recall that the street and sidewalk were being repaired. So a footprint is a possibility. But when you return to the scene, no footprints are left.

Then you remember that after the accident, the stranger leaned up against a store window. Perhaps he left some fingerprints. Ah, that might be the clue you need. So you look carefully, find those prints, take them to the Federal Bureau of Investigation, and the case is solved. Fingerprints help you find the good stranger, so everyone is happy.

About 2,000 years ago someone determined to save your life. Since Jesus Christ died on the cross, you can live forever. He left no footprints or fingerprints, but we can recognize him by the nail prints in his hands.

A disciple named Thomas did not believe that Jesus could be alive again. Even though he saw what appeared to be the living Lord, Thomas still wanted proof by seeing those nail prints in the hands of Jesus. And that is what happened. When Thomas saw Jesus, the risen Lord showed his hands to the doubting disciple. At last Thomas believed!

Now I Belong

Interest Object: Ring on finger

Main Truth: We can belong to others, but belonging to Jesus is best of all.

Scripture Text: Because you belong to Christ . . . (Mark 9:41 KJV).

I am glad that you accepted my invitation to come for the children's sermon today. You belong here with me. What a warm and wonderful feeling to be wanted and to belong. You are part of my special congregation here before the altar. I can call you "my" children and really mean it. So you belong to me. I am your pastor (or teacher).

But *I* also belong to someone else. Notice the ring on my left hand. That means I am married. My wife is here today. When we stood before the minister in church on our wedding day, we each gave the other a wedding ring. Anyone who sees these rings knows that we are married. We have promised to belong to each other as long as we both live here on earth. So I am happy to belong to my wife.

You are not old enough to be married, but you can still belong to many people and different groups. At school your teacher claims you. If you play soccer or any sport, you probably have a uniform with the name of your team. You belong to the Sonics or Pirates or whatever team where you play. You also belong to your parents who provide a home where you eat and sleep and play. But best of all, you can belong to Jesus.

In Mark 9:41, Jesus uses a phrase which expresses this idea. "Because you belong to Christ. . . ." What a happy thought. When we trust Jesus and invite him into our lives, he does not give us a ring. He gives us a new heart, a new life, new joy. We will never need to worry about death because heaven will be our home after death. We will live forever with Jesus in that happy place called heaven. How wonderful to belong to Jesus.

45

Strong Through Jesus

Interest Objects: Two large envelopes

Main Truth: Although we may be weak by ourselves, Jesus makes us strong.

Scripture Text: I can do all things in him who strengthens me (Phil. 4:13).

(Note: Ordinary envelopes made of paper are now being replaced by those made of new substances developed by chemical companies. You can purchase these new lighter weight envelopes from office supply companies. Many businesses also receive Priority Mail in these new envelopes provided to customers by the United States Postal Service. They will probably give you a used one from their trash can. Or just watch your mailbox and you are sure to recognize these improved versions.)

Here are a couple of ordinary envelopes which work hard delivering information through the mail. Let's look at this one made of paper first. Sometimes it can be accidentally torn or ripped. When that happens before the envelope arrives at its destination, the contents can be spilled or lost. I'll show you how easily this envelope is torn. (Rip!)

Here is another envelope which has been improved. It is very tough. Not even the strongest person here today can tear this envelope into little pieces. Watch as I try to poke my fist through it. (Pow!) No damage at all.

Sometimes an envelope gets wet and becomes so soft that it pulls apart. But not this new envelope. Water rolls off this envelope as easily as it rolls off a duck's back.

Why is this new envelope stronger? Because something special has been added to the paper. A chemical company can strengthen something ordinary by adding a plasticlike substance inside the fibers of paper. Then it becomes strong.

That is the way God works with us. In our own strength we are all very weak. But Jesus comes into our lives and helps us become strong. Then we can do things that we could have never done before—like being quiet on a rainy afternoon when your mother has a headache and can't stand noise. Normally you would make noise and get into trouble, but Jesus can help strengthen you so you can play quietly.

Paul explained this by saying "I can do all things in him who strengthens me." That means Jesus can help us with his special power to do anything.

46

Singing and Making Melody

Interest Object: Worship folder

Main Truth: A good leader helps us make better music for the Lord.

Scripture Text: Speaking to yourselves in psalms and hymns and spiritual songs, singing and making melody in your heart to the Lord (Eph. 5:19 KJV).

(Note: For this occasion a little preparation can do wonders to make the music minister or song leader look great. This person who leads music can have the choir ready with a simple presentation of "Jesus Loves Me." A few musical instruments such as a tambourine or a trumpet can add much.)

Children, I'm glad that you have come to worship today. You will notice that, like most churches, we have listed in our worship folder the songs we are going to sing. Many people call this a church bulletin. Whatever we call it, we like to sing the songs listed inside. Everyone loves music. It seems so easy. Some pastors wonder if leading the music could be more fun than preaching from the Bible.

Today, why don't we change leaders? I'm not prepared, but anyone should be able to sing. Would you children like for me to lead a song? Let's sing "Jesus Loves Me." Perhaps the choir would like to join us. You musicians at the piano and organ can help. Do we have any extra instruments of praise? Yes, I see a tambourine and a trumpet. You can join with us as we make melody to the Lord. Ready? Let's sing!

(If the choir members deliberately chose a different pitch with some instruments coming in too early or too late, bedlam will result. The music leader looks terribly embarrassed. The pastor's voice trails off in bewilderment. Finally, the music leader mercifully stops everything and explains what went wrong.)

"Pastor, I'm sorry. But something is wrong. Perhaps you haven't prepared for this music the way we music leaders practice before each worship service. We work with the musicians so that everyone knows how to begin. We must all be together so the congregation won't get confused. Could we all begin together? Everyone can follow my leadership as we fulfill Ephesians 5:19. But first, perhaps you might read to the children that favorite verse about singing. Then we can sing it right."

(Pastor reads verse. Then everyone sings "Jesus Loves Me." How good it sounds to make "melody in your heart to the Lord.")

47

Small Things

Interest Object: A penny

Main Truth: Little things in life can be very important.

Scripture Text: For who has despised the day of small things? (Zech. 4:10 NASB).

Here is the smallest coin in America. It is real money made by our government but it has very little value. Sometimes you can find a gumball machine that still accepts pennies. Or maybe even a parking meter on the street. But this penny is so little that most people will not even stop to pick one up from the sidewalk.

Merchants tell us that their customers do not like pennies. When they receive their change, many customers leave the pennies lying on the counter. So why does our government keep making pennies? Are these little coins any good at all?

Wait a minute. While these coins are little, that does not mean they are worthless. God sends us rain not in buckets or barrels but in little raindrops. With enough drops of rain, we can even have a flood.

Our buildings are held together by small nails. Writing is punctuated by small periods. Snow consists of countless little flakes of ice.

Would you want to play on a pile of sharp, big rocks? Not really. We prefer the soft sand on the beach. Yet the only difference between soft sand and hard rocks is the size of those stones. Big rocks would not feel good to our bare feet, but tiny rocks of sand are very comfortable to us.

Yes indeed, to be small like a penny is often better than being large. We ought never despise little things. Maybe nothing great is going to happen to you today. You don't have a birthday party scheduled or a trip to a park. But this day can still be a day of blessing through small accomplishments or little victories.

Let's be positive and happy. As Scripture says, "For who has despised the day of small things?"

48

The Invitation

Interest Object: A printed, formal invitation complete with envelope

Main Truth: God welcomes us all.

Scripture Text: The Spirit and the Bride say, "Come" (Rev. 22:17).

Everyone loves to receive mail. Here is an important looking envelope which appeared in my mailbox. It is an invitation to a wedding. Look how many words are engraved on this beautiful paper. It tells me who is inviting me, what the occasion is all about, when to come, whom I should call if I cannot come.

All of these words explain the invitation, but do you suppose it could be summarized into just one word? If we wanted to reduce this invitation to only one word, we could simply say "come."

Some people never associate God with that wonderful word. They think of God as an angry old man who points an accusing finger at guilty boys and girls to drive them away. But God loves us and wants to draw us close to his heart. So instead of shouting "Go away!" God whispers softly "Come to me."

This is one of God's favorite words. All through the Bible we find that God invites us into his presence. In the older part of the Bible known as the Old Testament, we have a wonderful invitation from God. "Come now, let us reason together, says the LORD: though your sins are like scarlet, they shall be as white as snow" (Isa. 1:18).

In the gospels Jesus invites us to "Come to me, all who labor and are heavy laden, and I will give you rest" (Matt. 11:28).

And what about the end of the Bible? In the last book called Revelation, we have this same idea of— you guessed it. It is a wedding invitation using that same, wonderful word again. "The Spirit and the Bride say, 'Come'" (Rev. 22:17).

Wedding ceremonies are happy celebrations. Everyone has a happy face. We meet nice people. At the reception we are served good food to eat. And it all begins with the invitation to come. God invites us to a party. I'm excited to think about all the fun we will have at that party in heaven.